Luke

The Gospel For All

Eric Dugan

ERG Ministry Resources provides materials for individuals and groups that is Evangelical, in the Reformed tradition and Grace-Driven while still seeking to be practical.

DEDICATION

Since one of my best friends in named Luke and as he is as
inquisitive as Dr. Luke, this one is for him.

CONTENTS

INTRODUCTION

Some people read the *New York Times*, others *USA Today* and others a blog or news website. They may all report the same events, but they do so in very different ways. One goes for depth, another may just hit the highpoints, while another may focus on the human side of the news. The Gospels are similar. Each writer brings a different perspective to the account of Jesus' earthly ministry. For Luke, his goal is clear:

"It seemed good to me also, having followed all things closely for some time past, to write an orderly account for you, most excellent Theophilus, that you may have certainty concerning the things you have been taught." (Luke 1:3-4)

We often joke that Presbyterians must always do everything decently and in order. If we had such things, Luke might be our patron saint. His gospel seeks to accurately record the facts of Jesus' ministry in a structured way in order to reinforce the faith of his readers. He writes his gospel and the book of Acts to Theophilus. This is a Greek name meaning "Lover or friend of God." It

1

may have been penned for a specific individual, but is also for any person who loves Jesus. It is particularly well-suited for Gentile believers who did not grow up in the faith. (Matthew, by contrast, is written to Jewish readers.) If you have unchurched kids, Luke is for you.

As you take up teaching this book, make sure you keep the focus on Jesus. Part of Doctor Luke's reason for being so meticulous is so that his readers would see Jesus in all of His glory. Don't mess that up. Let Jesus shine through your teaching.

The lessons are designed to be easy to use, but that doesn't mean don't prepare. I always recommend reading the sections ahead so you get the fuller context and so when James asks you about verse 50 and you are only going to verse 20 that lesson, you will, at least, have looked at it before. The lessons are also intentionally adaptable. If the illustration or activity isn't a good fit for your group, scrap it and do something that will work. Keep Luke's goal in mind and change the plan as you see fit.

As always—pray, pray, pray. Whether you are teaching established believers, new converts or non-believers, you do not have what it takes to impact their lives. God the Holy Spirit does, so invite Him into your group and "he will guide you into all the truth." (John 16:13a)

SESSION 1: HISTORY CLASS

Open: *Historic-* Share several stories. Are they real, historic events or myths? How can you tell?

Transition: Luke's gospel is presented as real history.

Read: Luke 1:1-4

The gospel is called Luke because he was the author of both this and the book of Acts. So who is he? Interestingly, he wasn't one of the disciples like Matthew, Mark & John. He is actually a doctor.

Read: Colossians 4:14

He was probably a gentile who accompanied Paul on his second missionary journey and afterward.

So how did he end up writing a gospel?

Each gospel has its own flavor. Matthew is aimed at Jewish readers and shows how Jesus fulfills prophecies. Mark is the "immediate" gospel. It hits the high points and moves quickly through the narrative. John, one of Jesus closest friends, provides a warm, eyewitness account. Luke is more of a history. As a doctor, Luke was very precise and wanted to include info and details that the others did not.

This is real history, carefully researched and recorded. Unlike myths or tall tales, he includes details which can and have been verified outside of the text. For instance: sceptics questioned whether Pontius Pilate actually existed. Archeological finds have since proven his existence and the approximate dates of his rule.

Luke compiled his account by listening to numerous eyewitnesses and researching the details. It was written within 30 years of Christ's crucifixion, so many witnesses were still alive.

So why bother? What purpose is there for this gospel?

He wanted believers to have certainty that they weren't taught lies or fables.

Read: Vs 4

And like John, it was so that people might meet Jesus and believe in Him.

Read: John 20:30-31

Closing: This book is a history, but more importantly, an introduction to Jesus.

Historic or Not?

Italics=untrue

1. Albert Einstein, himself a Jew, was offered the position of president of Israel in 1952, but declined.

2. The modern cellphone was actually adapted from captured alien technology from Roswell.

3. St. Nicholas was a Prussian general who converted to Christianity and was known, as a young man, to have had a pet reindeer.

4. George Washington had wooden dentures.

5. In 1807, to celebrate the end of a war with Russia, Napoleon Bonaparte wanted to have a rabbit hunt. His chief of staff Berthier was charged with gathering the rabbits. Upon their release, they attacked the men and the men had to flee.

6. Andrew Jackson had a pet parrot named Poll who broke into swear words at his funeral in 1845.

7. Peter Pan came out of author J.M. Barrie's friendship with Sylvia Llewelyn Davies. He told stories to amuse her children, one of whom was named Peter.

8. Hercules was the son of Zeus/Juno, and had amazing strength.

2 MUTE WITNESS

Open: *Charades*- Have volunteers try to communicate important info without using words. (See examples on the following page.)

Transition: Imagine how hard it would be to communicate big news if you couldn't use words. That's where Zechariah found himself.

Read: Luke 1:5-24

Zechariah was a Levite. Because there were so many of them, they didn't all serve at the temple at the same time. During this rotation, he had been selected to light the incense in the temple.

While he was serving, an angel appeared to him and gave him great news. Despite his wife being barren and both of them being old, they would have a child.

Does that remind you of anyone? God often demonstrates His power in this way.

Read: Genesis 17:16-19

Abraham and Sarah had a similar situation and God gave them a son who was very special.

Zechariah and Elizabeth would have a special son, too.

He was to be named John. We typically know him as John the Baptist to differentiate between him and the apostle John. (The author of the gospel of John.)

What was extra special about this boy? (Vs 15-16 say he will be great before the Lord; filled with the Holy Spirit; he will lead a revival; he would have a role like Elijah; he would prepare the way for the Lord's coming.) It was almost like being on *the Price is Right*. In the Showcase Showdown they start with something small like a toaster and keep adding more amazing things as each curtain is pulled back. Elizabeth and Zechariah would have been happy with a healthy child, but got so much more.

Like Abraham and Sarah, though, there is doubt. So the priest asks Gabriel about it. The angel gives him a sign, though probably not the one he wanted. He is struck mute.

Can you imagine having great news, but not being able to share it?

You know what is amazing about this? He ended up being a witness to the God's power even without speaking. The people saw that something had happened and knew it was of the Lord.

We have great news to share with our world. We get to use our words, but it is important that we testify with our lives, too. Like Zechariah, we can give glory to God by faithfully living for Him.

Closing: You've got great news. Don't be afraid to share it.

Charades:

Without using words see if you can get others to understand this important info.

I'm having a baby!

I got a new job.

I got my driver's license.

I'm choking.

I'm getting married.

The food is poisoned.

I have to go to the bathroom.

3 ORIGIN STORY

Open: *Origin Stories-* Super-heroes and others often have origin stories about how they became who they are. Can you guess who each person is by their origin story? (See the following page.)

Transition: Luke 1-2 provides some of the "origin story" of how Jesus took on flesh in order to be our savior.

Read: Luke 1:26-38, Luke 2:1-7

The Christmas story is repeated at least once a year. That can sometimes mean that we don't always pay close attention, but we probably should. Luke includes more detail in his version that the other gospel writers. Part of that relates to Mary.

Put yourself, for a moment, in her shoes. She was a young woman–probably in her teens, who was engaged to be married. There is nothing particularly special about her. She seems to be quite ordinary. That is, until an angel visits her.

What does he tell her? (Despite being a virgin, she will bear a child who is the Son of God.)

How freaked out would you be? It had to be really humbling to discover that you had been chosen to bear and raise the Son of God, but also terrifying. Furthermore, she had to explain this whole virgin birth thing to her husband-to-be and deal with the gossip and shame of people thinking she had been unfaithful to him.

Amazingly, she goes with it. She has a similar attitude to Jesus Himself.

Read: Matthew 26:39

She didn't have to understand how it was possible or even why God would choose her, she just submitted to His will.

God uses ordinary people to do amazing things for Him.

Her faith sets the stage for the birth account.

Jesus, though worthy of the trappings of a king, was born as an outsider, under a cloud of shame amid the farm animals.

Bethlehem was not Mary & Joseph's home. They were only there because of a census, so Jesus was born as something of an outsider.

He was definitely born under a cloud of shame.

Did you ever wonder why anyone would send a heavily pregnant woman to go sleep in a barn? Couldn't they have found someplace for her?

When good Jewish folks saw this young couple, they may have seen them as sinners who were having a baby out of wedlock. Worse yet, the child was not Joseph's. (Luke 2:7 emphasizes that Jesus was "*her* firstborn son," not "their firstborn son.") It was uncomfortable, so it was easier to send them away. Because of a Hebrew tradition of hospitality to travelers, however, something was done and the stables/animal areas were offered.

So Jesus was born among the animals. It seems appropriate, however, as these creatures may have been the ones used in sacrifices. Jesus was born to be our sacrifice.

Read: Hebrews 10:4-7

And His was the only sacrifice that can truly save us.

Closing: God used an ordinary woman of faith to bring us the savior we needed. Rejoice that she endured the shame that Jesus might bear yours.

Origin Story

Can you tell who it is just by their origin story?

1. He was bitten by a radioactive spider. (Spiderman)

2. They were exposed to cosmic radiation during a space flight. (The Fantastic Four)

3. He was born in Asgard, the son of Odin. (Thor)

4. She was trained to be a spy and assassin in Russia. (Black Widow)

5. She grew up as Stephani Germanotta and learned to play music. (Lady Gaga)

6. She was born an Amazon princess. (Wonder Woman)

7. He supposedly cut down a cherry tree. (George Washington)

8. He was exposed to Gamma radiation (Hulk)

9. His parents sent him away from their home planet just before it exploded. (Superman)

10. His wealthy parents were murdered by a street thug in an alley. (Batman)

11. After his mother's death, he was sent to live with his aunt & uncle on a desert planet named Tatooine. (Luke Skywalker)

12. Before encountering a precious magic ring, he was just a plain old Hobbit. (Gollum)

13. He was given experimental Super Soldier Serum during World War 2. (Captain America)

14. She was a mutant born in Africa and could control weather. (Storm)

15. He was a mutant born with healing powers and claws. (Wolverine)

4 WHO INVITED THEM?

Open: *Least Deserving Awards*- Who least deserves the given award? Such as Best actor, singer, driver, humanitarian, etc.

Transition: Even though they might not deserve it, sometimes those people do win. Today some smelly folks get what they don't deserve.

Read: Luke 2:8-20

When you hear that passage, it is hard not to think of *A Charlie Brown Christmas*. (You may wish to show the cli) It is Linus' way of making it clear what Christmas is all about.

The presence of the shepherds drives that point home.

What do you know about shepherds? If you were looking at future careers, do you think shepherd would be on it? Why not?

In fact, shepherds were often the youngest family

member or those who could do little else. It was a terrible job. Sheep are so dumb that you had to watch them all the time. That meant sleeping with them. As a result, shepherds were not usually very clean. They didn't get invited to parties and were usually looked down upon.

Can you think of a career today that people might think of the same way? (Fast food worker, trash man, etc.?)

In His coming, Jesus was proving He was going to be doing something different than other kings. Instead of a royal reception with dignitaries and important people, He invited shepherds.

Why do you think He did so?

Because that is exactly who He came for. He came to save the unclean, the least of these.

Read: Luke 19:10

The shepherds had to be amazed to be singled out, so once they heard, they responded immediately. They high-tailed it to Bethlehem to see the child they were told about. You know what they did after that? They told everybody.

In our social media-obsessed world, we share about everything. If we got an extra Chicken McNugget, it's Snap worthy; if the barista spells our name right, it's a post. These folks had something really important to share, and amazingly, people listened. After-all, if God would speak to the lowest, might He not speak to them, too?

In a sense, we were there at the birth of Jesus through our representatives, the shepherds. Like them, we are unclean. We have nothing in us that deserves to be loved by God and yet He calls us. And when He calls, we respond immediately. Once you have known His forgiveness and grace, you can't help but tell others. We are the shepherds.

Closing: Jesus came for you and He invites you to respond in faith and follow Him.

5 HOME ALONE

Open: *The Teen Years*- Have you ever wondered what famous figures were like as teens? We all know about Anne Frank because of her diary, but what about Churchill? Lincoln? Washington? (Share some fun facts or do as a quiz. Some samples are included on the following page.)

Transition: Our childhood often impacts who we are as adults. What was Jesus' youth like?

Read: Luke 2:40-52

There is very little information about Jesus as a boy. When last we saw him, he was a young child in his parents' home in Nazareth. (Matthew 2:23.) It has been several years since then. We don't get the details about his education, childhood friends or anything else. We next see him as a preteen.

Can you think of ages when special things happen in your life? For instance—what happens at 16? (Sweet 16, driver's license.) 18? (Vote, considered an adult.) 15? (In

Latin cultures, Quinceañera.) What was special about 13 for Jewish children? (They were considered to have reached manhood/womanhood as signified by the bar mitvah and bat mitzvah ceremonies.)

Jesus is now 12. While it might seem young to us, he was almost at the age where he would be considered in many ways as a adult. He could be apprenticed in a career and could actually leave his parent's home to be on his own, if He chose. His family may have traveled to Jerusalem in preparation for this ceremony and to observe the Passover.

This road trip goes slightly awry when the family decides to head home. They all leave, but Jesus remains behind.

How did that happen?

If you are from a bigger family, have you ever been left behind somewhere? Maybe one parent thought the other was picking you up after practice? At this time, families traveled together in large groups–grandparents, cousins, uncles and aunts. There may have been dozens of people traveling with Mary & Joseph and their other younger children. Oftentimes, the women and children left first with the men joining later. At 12, Jesus would fit in either group, so each probably thought He was with the other.

It might seem that Jesus was rebelliously staying behind in the big city, but He was simply in His father's house sitting with the teachers. This was almost like *Home Alone*– they left him behind.

What do you do in moments of uncertainty? Complain? Worry? Freak out?

Jesus turns to His Father.

That was His custom throughout His earthly life.

Read: Mark 1:35, Luke 9:18

So it is no surprise that He does the same here.

When Mary & Joseph locate Him, they are perturbed and lash out at him. Notice Jesus' reaction? It is calm and factual, not confrontational. Even though His parents are wrong, He doesn't attack them.

Read: Exodus 20:12

Keeping this commandment includes when your parent is wrong. Jesus got that and submitted to their will.

And like the rest of us, He continued to grow up in all areas of His life.

Closing: This account is included for a reason. It reminds us of how to deal with uncertainty and how to grow as a person of faith.

Fun Facts:

Lincoln:

Though born in Kentucky, Lincoln was raised in rural Hurricane Township in Southern Indiana.

His mother died when he was 9.

He had very little formal education and mostly learned from his own reading.

As a young man he worked as boatman, store clerk, surveyor and militia soldier.

Washington:

He was one of 10 children born to a wealthy family.

He did not much enjoy studying literature, reading or language studies.

At 16 he took his first job as a surveyor.

He invested the funds he made in buying tracts of land. He owned 1500 acres by the time he was 21.

6 YOU HAD ONE JOB

Open: *You Had One Job-* Share several pics of people who messed up on a simple task. (Many examples are available online.)

How embarrassing would it be to be the person who had one thing to do and ended up doing it badly?

Transition: Jesus' cousin John has one basic job to do. Did he do it well?

Read: Luke 3:1-22

Quick note: The gospels are accurate histories. Note Luke's careful listing of the various officials and their territories.

John was born miraculously to Elizabeth and Zechariah despite Elizabeth being unable to have children. He is now grown up and serving the Lord. What job does God call him to do? (Prepare the way for the Lord.)

If you were preparing for a party what would you have

to do? For Christmas? Graduation?

Usually such events have a certain pomp and circumstance. Preparing for the messiah is a bit different. The main job John had was to show people their sin and their need for a savior.

Instead of wrapping gifts, picking a menu or blowing up balloons, John had to approach people with the dark truth of who they are.

Read: Romans 3:23

We know we fall short, but this was a radical idea to many of the Jewish leaders. They thought they were okay. They followed the ceremonial laws, were circumcised, didn't eat bacon, etc. Most importantly–they were Jews, not pagans. Why should they worry about sin?

Despite their reservations, many of the common folks responded. Why do you think that was? (They knew they were sinners.)

John's baptism was one of repentance. *It is not the same as Christian baptism.* It is a transitional rite preparing people for the messiah.

You may not have realized this, but the Jews practiced several kinds of baptisms from sprinkling the altar and its tools to the baptism of Gentiles who wished to convert. (The first were part of Old Testament law, while the last one was a Jewish custom.)

John was just applying something similar except to Jewish people who wished to outwardly show their repentance. That was only part of the story, though. He needed them to see their sin, so that they could then see

Jesus.

John's baptism was a turning from something (Sin); Christian baptism is a turning to something. (Jesus.) The sacrament symbolizes our association with the completed work of Christ and being a part of His covenant body. John made it clear that Jesus' baptism was way better than what he could offer.

So why did Jesus get baptized? He had nothing of which to repent.

Read: Matthew 3:13-15

Matthew says it was to fulfill all righteousness. Scholars debate the meaning, but it may have been because He was to be our representative and was standing, as it were, in our place.

Regardless, God is pleased and all three persons of the trinity appear in order to show their approval.

Closing: John had one job: prepare the way for the Lord. He accomplished that task by pointing the people to one who was greater than he. You can be like John and do the same by pointing folks to Jesus.

7 THAT'S TEMPTING

Open: *Temptation–* What food would you find really tempting? What kind of things would you want to eat even if you were already stuffed? (Pizza, ice cream, cheesecake, etc.) Is there a food that would be no temptation whatsoever? (Tofu, lima beans, spinach?) Why? What if you were starving and hadn't eaten in days?

Transition: Jesus faced such a temptation.

Read: Luke 4:1-12

We don't do this as much today, but people used to do fasting more often. That meant going without food for a period of time. Why might people do such a thing? (To focus on prayer, to cleanse the body, to overcome a controlling behavior.)

Jesus fasted during a time of severe temptation.

The Spirit led Him out into the wilderness, away from all of the distractions of life, in order to go one-on-one with Satan.

What does Satan tempt Him with? (Food, power and proving God's love.) You notice he doesn't try tofu or being beaten with sticks. He picks things people might legitimately want.

Read: Hebrews 4:15

Satan typically uses good things to tempt us with. He just wants to use them in a bad way.

Can you think of things that he can use like that? (Sex, honor, money, food, pleasure, etc. Have students brainstorm how Satan might tempt them or their peers with good things.)

For example: Sex is a great gift of God, but it is to be used in the context of marriage. Satan can tempt us to claim that good gift with someone we aren't married to, through pornography or through sexual behaviors that stop shy of intercourse.

Knowing that Jesus was hungry, Satan suggested Jesus turn stones to bread. Why do you think Jesus said no? After-all, He had a legitimate need. (Answers may vary.)

There were things far more important than food at that moment. Jesus knew the Lord would sustain Him.

The next is one we encounter a lot: Getting things the easy way even if it isn't the right way.

Have you ever faced that kind of temptation? Perhaps by cheating on a test, cutting corners at your job, getting someone to like you by lying about someone else?

Satan was offering Jesus a way to have power without

sacrifice. He was giving Him an option to bypass the cross.

The last strikes at the heart: Does God really love you? Can you really trust Him?

In each circumstance, where did Jesus turn? (The Word of God.)

Read: 1 Corinthians 10:13

There is always a way out. The best is to lean into God and His Word. Jesus is showing us how to deal with the temptations we face.

Closing: As you are tempted this week, remember Jesus and turn to the Lord instead of giving in. (And if you mess up, do exactly the same to find His forgiveness and love.)

8 TO DO LIST

Open: *To Do List-* What do you have to do this week? What are things you might put on a to do list? What fun things would you like to have on that list? Many people write such checklists in order to make sure they do all that needs to be done.

Transition: What do you think was on Jesus' to do list? He gives us a peek at some of it today.

Read: Luke 4:16-30

What happens when a missionary is in town? Don't they usually say a few words at the worship time? Perhaps do a presentation during Sunday School?

In Jesus' day, it was customary for visiting teachers or rabbis to visit the synagogue and be prepared to share with the group. Jesus was doing that. He was given a scroll to read and He selected a portion to share. As was the custom, He then sat down to teach and field questions.

What He read amounted to a "to do list" for the

Messiah. What things does Isaiah point to? (Ministry to the poor, freeing captives, healing the blind, freeing the oppressed and proclaiming the year of the Lord's favor.)

That's a lot of stuff to accomplish. How did the people react? (They liked it.) They were excited to think about Jesus healing, freeing, blessing them.

But then Jesus kept talking.

These blessings weren't for them. Why?

He recounts the stories of Elijah and Elisha. They ministered powerfully to a widow and a leper, but they did not do the same for every widow and leper.

There is one thing that marked them as different from, perhaps, others. They knew they had a problem and that they couldn't solve it. They had no hope but in the Lord.

That's something the Pharisees didn't get and neither did many in Nazareth.

Read: Matthew 9:12-13

They didn't realize they were spiritually sick. Their problems were far deeper than just poverty, political oppression or illness. They needed a savior. And instead of embracing Jesus, they sought to kill him.

Despite all of that–He still had things to do. Their lack of faith would not stop His work. He immediately started doing just what He said He would do.

Read: Luke 4:30-44

He freed the oppressed, healed the sick and proclaimed

the good news.

Closing: Jesus is still doing the work of Messiah. Have you realized your own helplessness and need of a savior and turned to Him to find peace?

9 A FEW LESS THAN GOOD MEN

Open: *Qualifications-* What does it take to be eligible to do the given task? (Such as: Drive a car, go to college, get married, be a surgeon, take Algebra 2, play division 1 sports, etc.)

Transition: When Jesus was looking for helpers, He opted to appoint seemingly less qualified men.

Read: Luke 5:1-11

Simon (Peter), James & John were fishermen. What do you know about this job? (Have you seen an episode of *Deadliest Catch*, for instance.)

This was a back-breaking career with long hours and lots of opportunity for failure. The men who did this job were often a bit rough around the edges and not terribly educated. That's a fact that the people noticed about the disciples later in their ministry.

Read: Acts 4:13

So why pick them? (Answers will vary.)

It's worth thinking about: Just what does it take to be a disciple?

Do you have to be smart? Educated? Well-connected? Have your life together? Be kind? Loving?

Those are all great things, but is that what Jesus is looking for?

Read: Vs 5

Simon has faith. He doesn't understand Jesus' request and can argue that he knows more about fishing than his carpenter friend, but he does it anyway. He believes Jesus.

That is what it takes to be a disciple: Faith in Jesus. That's it. Nothing more and nothing less.

And that was true of the others who were called. (Except for Judas Iscariot.)

Read: Luke 6:13-16

Jesus can use men like them, and He can use you, too, if you have faith.

Isn't that great news? You don't have to be perfectly holy or extremely knowledgeable to be used by the Lord. He can still do great things through you.

He turned fishermen into fishers of men. Within a few years, they saw thousands come to faith through their preaching. It was all because of the Spirit's equipping.

Closing: If you have faith in Jesus, you are qualified as a disciple and He will use you for His glory.

10 WHAT DO YOU NEED?

Open: *Greater Than, Less Than-* Some things are easy to figure out. 5 is greater than 2, for instance, but what about in other areas? Which is worth more to you-- time or money? Having a relationship or a high GPA? Playing a sport or having a job? Relationship with your parents or having more freedom? A fancy dinner out or pizza in the living room? Have those priorities ever changed?

Transition: Some men come to Jesus seeking what they think is the best thing, but leave with something even better.

Read: Luke 5:17-25

First some basics: Homes were different in that region than in our own. They were often rectangular with flat roofs. As rains were infrequent, they didn't have to be as weather tight as our own, so they may have been some rough timbers with a few branches and a layer of mud, thatch or tile. There were usually stairs or a ladder to access the roof which was used for various functions. (Including bathing, as Bathsheba proved.) That means it wasn't terribly odd to find people able to bring a paralyzed man to the roof. (You may wish to show a picture of such a building. Many are available in Bible Atlases or online.)

Have you ever had one of those moments—perhaps in class, when you weren't really paying attention but then you got called on and end up answering the wrong question? For instance, they asked: "What is your favorite character in the story?" and you say, "11:45," because you thought they asked for the time.

That almost seems like that is what is happening here. These guys clearly went to all this trouble because they had heard Jesus could heal people. They rip out a roof and lower their obviously paralyzed friend down to Jesus and it seems like He doesn't get it. Instead of healing him, Jesus forgives his sins.

This man has what we call a "felt need." Felt needs are those we know we have—like hunger, thirst, desire for love, etc. Sometimes, we have deeper needs we aren't as aware of. For instance, a person might have a felt need to be a starter on their team, but discover during the sports physical that they have a medical condition that needs immediate attention. That is a greater need.

So Jesus addresses the man's deeper need.

Read: Vs 20

These guys had the gift of faith already, so Jesus meets their greatest need by granting forgiveness.

That, of course, riled up the Pharisees, for they rightly knew that was something only God could do.

Jesus then addresses the man's more obvious felt

need, too, by healing him. That act served to prove that Jesus could actually do the first thing.

Forgiving sins was much harder. Why? (Jesus had to die to do that, but could heal with just a touch or a word.) That's even true for us. It is often harder to forgive someone who has hurt us than to give money or sacrifice our time. Forgiveness, however, is much more important.

Closing: Your felt needs will change over time. Some will be met; some will not, but the greatest needs you have has already been met by Jesus. Rejoice in that.

11 MISSING THE POINT

Open: *Bad Cliff Notes-* Read bad summaries that completely miss the point of a well-known book or movie. (See following page for examples.)

Transition: Sometimes you can't see the forest for the trees. The Pharisees sure missed the point of God's commands.

Read: Luke 6:1-11

Have you ever done that– completely missed the point of something? It may have been that you missed the signals that a member of the opposite sex was interested in you or even something more basic like that you misunderstood a Math concept.

The Pharisees were so obsessed with achieving righteousness in their own power that they ended up creating all kinds of additional rules about everything.

They were enraged about Jesus and the Sabbath. Let's look at what the actual Sabbath command was.

Read: Exodus 20:8-11

What is the basic idea here? (Rest from your job and honor God with the day.) The main idea seems to be that God is blessing His people with a day off and the opportunity to fellowship with Him. It has more of the idea of: It's a snow day. Since there's no school, you get to go hang out with your friend Billy.

The Pharisees, instead, focused on what you *could not do*, rather than the blessings of what you could do.

Let's look at what they objected to.

Read: Vs. 1-2

The disciples were hungry and were, in accordance with the law, eating a bit of grain as they walked through a field. The Pharisees objected because they considered rubbing the grain to remove the husk to be equal to threshing, which was work.

That is like equating lifting your spoon to eat Jell-o with using a backhoe.

Did Jesus violate Exodus 20? (No.) He violated the rules of men who had *no authority* to make such rules.

The next section was even more bizarre.

Read: Vs 9-10

How would normal people react to seeing a man miraculously healed from a life-long infirmity? (They would be amazed, rejoice, congratulate the man, thank the healer, etc.)

Instead of glorifying God at this act that only He could accomplish, they go after Jesus. They called this healing work.

Again—did this violate Exodus 20? (Still no.)

They thoroughly missed the point. They focused on their own rules and couldn't see the Lord as a result.

Closing: We often pile on the Pharisees because they focused so much on their own ideas that they missed the big picture, but we do the same. We become so fixated on our own interests or favorite ideas, that we miss how the Lord is working in other areas. This passage reminds us that we, too, need to keep our eyes on Jesus.

Read: Hebrews 12:1-2

Bad Cliff Notes:

What work is being summarized. . . badly?

It's a book about sticking stuff in trees. *(To Kill a Mockingbird)*

It's the story of the majestic architecture, fashion and hairstyles of the Capitol. *(The Hunger Games)*

A cookbook for Second Breakfasts. *(Lord of the Rings)*

The story of how paper is made and sold. *(The Office.)*

A paranormal investigation of holiday specters. *(A Christmas Carol)*

A cruise guide of the places to see along the Mississippi River. *(Huck Finn)*

A study of the creepy flirtatious relationship between a twin brother and sister, one of who is on the lighter side. *(Star Wars)*

How to win friends and influence people in ancient Rome. *(Julius Caesar)*

Saying goodnight to a red balloon. *(Goodnight Moon)*

12 NOT WORTHY

Open: *Humble Brag-* Have you ever heard that phrase? What does it mean? (Someone says something in a seemingly humble way, but is really bragging.) Share several examples. (Some can be found here: https://twistedsifter.com/2011/05/funniest-humble-brags-on-twitter/.)

Transition: Do you like people who brag about themselves? The man we meet today might have reason to brag, but he remains humble.

Read: Luke 7:1-10

Have you had that moment in your life yet when you were awesome at something, but then you met someone who is so much more talented in that area that you realize you really weren't the greatest of all time? For example: In the second season of *Stranger Things*, Dustin discovers that a new student, Mad Max, has set the new high scores on all of the video games at the arcade. He was good, but she was better.

The centurion is in such a situation. By all accounts, he was an honorable man. The Jewish leaders clearly thought very highly of him and he had several things of which to be proud. But he knows that he pales by comparison with Jesus.

Yet, he loves his servant. It saddens him that this one is ill and possibly close to death. So he swallows his pride and asks Jesus for help.

Here's what is amazing about this account: He has greater faith than the Jews!

He knew he was unworthy, despite what the leaders said. He also believed so strongly in Jesus that he knew Jesus didn't actually have to touch the servant to heal him.

Out of love for this man, Jesus did as he asked and healed that servant without a touch.

Sometimes, however, Jesus did touch as He healed.

Read: Luke 7:11-17

This was another group of humble people. This widow knew she had nothing and no earthly hope. Her only son was dead. Jesus reached out to touch his dead body.

You know why this was odd?

Normally if you contacted a dead body, you were rendered ceremonially unclean. But Jesus touches him anyway and instead makes the unclean clean with his touch.

The man is restored to life and everyone marvels at

the power of God.

Closing: We all come to Jesus unworthy of His love and forgiveness, but thankfully, He loves the unworthy.

13 SHE LOVES MUCH

Open:

Option 1: Sleuthing- Detectives and forensics experts look at a crime scene to try to piece together what led to the result. Can you determine, from the results, what the cause was for these mysteries? (See *Mini Mysteries* on the following page.)

Transition: Today we will try to deduce what causes a woman to treat Jesus the way she does.

Option 2: Effect & Cause- Bring in several examples of effects (Such as a bowl containing the results of mixing baking soda & vinegar, a burned piece of paper, a cupcake, a report card, etc.). Can they figure out what caused this result? (Ex. Putting a match to paper, mixing cake mix.)

Transition: Today we will see what effect results from being forgiven by Jesus.

Read: Luke 7:36-50

Have you ever been invited to a fancy dinner? What

customs are usually followed? (Such as etiquette, dress code, acceptable behaviors, etc.)

Jesus has been invited to eat with a Pharisee. This would have been a more formal affair. As was the custom, people ate at a low table while reclining on floor pillows. That's all pretty ordinary.

What happens next is not. A woman who is a well-known sinner bursts in and starts anointing Jesus feet with expensive perfume while weeping and drying his feet with her hair.

There is some debate about this, but this was likely Martha and Lazarus' sister Mary. (The debate being that this may have happened more than once in Jesus' ministry.)

Read: John 11:2, 12:3

All we are told is that this woman was a notorious sinner. The Pharisee is amazed Jesus would let her anywhere near Him as a result.

So Jesus tells a story about debts forgiven. The one who has been forgiven more displays greater love and thankfulness.

Don't get confused here, though: Love is a *result* of being forgiven, *not the cause* of it.

Like us, she is saved by faith in Jesus.

Read: Vs. 50

Because she got the gospel, she knew herself to be a sinner who deserved judgment. She also knew Jesus loved her and forgave her. Her response reflects that.

Illustration: When people are rescued from disasters, they often cling to their rescuers. They understand how close to death they were and appreciate more fully the people who came to help them.

Here's the interesting thing about this account that the host didn't get: Mary wasn't the greatest sinner in that room. The Pharisee was.

Yes—he was more outwardly holy, but because of that, he couldn't see his own lack of faith. He wasn't showing love to Jesus because he really didn't think he needed a savior. The effect of that is coldness toward Jesus.

Closing: Which is closer to you? Mary or the Pharisee? Do you get your sin and stand amazed that God still loves you or are you resting in your own righteousness?

Mini Mysteries:

Case 1: Mr. Sanders is found on the living room floor dead. There is a gunshot wound in his chest. The gun matches Mr. Sander's registered firearm. A note on the table is addressed to "my sweetie" and is signed, "Your Pooh bear, Kiki." Mrs. Sanders name is Cheryl. The house is empty, but the keys to his wife's Mitsubishi are missing, as is his wallet. There is no sign of forced entry and no other items were disturbed.

(Mrs. Sanders discovered her husband was having an affair and shot him.)

Case 2: Ezekiel goes to the doctor. His heart is racing and he appears jumpy and slightly irritated. His blood pressure is a little high, but his other vitals are normal. He is wearing comfortable clothes and shoes, is not using a cell phone and has an empty cup of Starbuck's coffee with him. He reports no extraordinary stress in his life.

(These symptoms can be caused by too much caffeine.)

Case 3: There is trash strewn across the kitchen floor. Mr. Bigsley, your beagle, is sleeping contentedly in the corner. The family is definitely not vegan.

(The dog got into the trash to eat scraps.)

14 RESULTS WILL VARY

Open: *Chemistry Experiments-* Do the same experiment twice, but change one element the second time. How does it impact the result? (Vinegar & baking soda and water & baking soda; make an egg float in salt water but sink in plain water or Diet Coke & Mentos and Sprite & Mentos.)

Transition: A little change can make a big difference.

Read: Luke 8:4-15

The teacher lectures or the coach instructs. Everybody gets the exact same material. Then why do some go on to get A's or become the leading scorer while others fail the test or sit the bench?

People are all different. That's something that Jesus points to in this parable. The Word goes out but impacts folks differently. That makes sense to us because we all know people who grew up in the church and continue to follow Jesus and others who walked away from Him. It helps us to understand why that is.

Ultimately, this story about a farmer is actually an encouragement to the disciples. The success of their ministry does not depend on them. They are merely to spread the gospel and let it have its effect.

Read: 1 Corinthians 3:6-7

It is God who saves, not the sower. Since we are not God, we don't know what will happen with the good news we bring. Some will reject it; some will accept it for a time but when hardships come, they will turn to other things; but some will believe and flourish. We must trust God to do His work.

While the parable was an encouragement for the disciples, it was also a challenge to the other hearers. Which soils were they? Were they open to the Word? Were they just in it for the short-term?

Some were, no doubt, like the men of Athens Paul encountered.

Read: Acts 17:21

Those looking for the latest idea would not stick with Jesus.

Closing: Has God transformed you from clay to rich soil? Are you growing in Him?

15 SUPPER TIME

Open: *Dinner Party-* Plan a festive menu for a dinner party. What would you serve? How many guests might you invite? What would the decorations be like? Music?

Transition: Would it change things if you were serving 100? 500? Or even 5,000?

Read: Luke 9:10-17

Full disclosure—some folks read this account differently. Liberal theologians start from a supposition that miracles can't exist, so when stories like this appear, they have to come up with non-miraculous explanations. The most popular is "stone soup." In their viewing, the people really did have food, but they didn't want others to know it. After a little boy gave up his lunch (John 6:9), that inspired them to offer up the items they had hidden. So the story is about sharing.

That is not what happened. This account is given in all 4 gospels for a reason and the miraculous is why.

The people had come out to hear Jesus and to be healed. As the day went on, the disciples realized the people would need to have food and lodging soon. The practical solution was to send them home. (By the way, there would have been no shame in people eating their own provisions, if they had had them.)

Jesus had another solution. He told the disciples to feed them. But they saw that all they had was a few small loaves of bread and a couple of fish. For Jesus, that wasn't a problem. He took the small cache of food and multiplied it to feed all and even have leftovers.

So why did He do this? Why not just send them home? (Answers will vary.)

There are multiple reasons. For one–Jesus loved them. He cared about not just their spiritual needs, but their physical ones, too. He would provide for them.

Recall the Lord's prayer?

Read: Matthew 6:11

We pray for our daily needs because God desires to take care of them.

There was something deeper going on as well, and it involved the disciples.

Jesus had asked them to feed the crowds and they lacked the faith to do so. By doing this miracle, He is reminding them of who He is and what He has empowered them to do.

It is significant that there were 12 disciples and 12 baskets of left-overs. Each now had food to give to others.

They could do what Jesus asked.

Closing: God cares about your needs and He can equip you to bless others, too.

16 HOW MUCH?

Open: *How Much?* Show several items. (From a can of beans to a piece of jewelry.) What would you pay for the given item? How much would be too much to pay? Could you actually pay that price?

Transition: Jesus calls on His followers to consider the cost of following Him.

Read: Luke 9:23-27, 57-62

Few people think much before buying a candy bar or a Starbuck's drink, but when it comes to big things, they give it lots of thought. For instance-- before buying a car or house or investing tens of thousands of dollars in a college education. When it matters, we think about it.

Why do you think Jesus had this conversation with His followers? (Answers will vary.)

We can often forget that the disciples did not know about the cross at this point. They would have known about the Romans' usage of it as a penalty, but not about their friend Jesus eventually dying on it.

So this may have been a confusing conversation for them. What did "take up your cross" mean to them?

They probably didn't think about physical death as much as metaphorically dying to self. Jesus presents it as following Him.

He discusses it again in Luke 14.

Read: Luke 14:25-33

What is the cost of following Jesus?

The journey of faith begins by acknowledging our own insufficiency. We are sinners and we can't save ourselves. So part of the cost is recognizing that, getting over yourself and fully trusting in Jesus.

But what other costs might there be to following Jesus?

For example: (You can share personal stories, too.)

1. You may get made fun of as a goody-two-shoes or viewed as holier than thou if you seek to live out your faith.

2. You may have fewer sexual partners than others if you choose to follow the scripture's admonitions and restrict sexual activity to within the bonds of marriage.

3. You will have to trust and follow your spiritual leaders even when they may not always come up with the best solutions.

4. You may not advance as far in your career since you will not be as willing to do less ethical things.

What costs have you experienced?

There is a reason Jesus calls upon His followers to consider these things before becoming His disciples. Remember the parable of the soils? Some who didn't take that time end up departing when the difficulties of life came upon them.

Closing: Have you considered the cost? If so, remember that Jesus never leaves His own. No matter what price you pay for being His disciple, He is right there with you!

17 HOW TO

Open: *How-To Guides-* Hand out several simple how-to guides for things such as making a paper plane, (https://sites.google.com/site/paperairplaneinstructionsyuy/ or https://paperairplaneshq.com/paper-airplanes.html) folding a sheet, (https://www.marthastewart.com/269141/how-to-fold-a-fitted-sheet) drawing a bunny, (https://www.wikihow.com/Draw-a-Bunny) etc. After reading it, could you do it?

Transition: The disciples wanted to know how to pray, so Jesus gave them a how-to guide.

Read: Luke 11:1-13

When you are young, you have to learn how to do everything–feed yourself, use the potty, read and write. They want to do what they see others doing. These young disciples hear Jesus praying and they realize they really don't know how to do it.

Though we often refer to this as the Lord's Prayer, it

is actually the disciples' prayer. Do you think Jesus wanted them to repeat this prayer only? Why not?

It is a model prayer that they can use to help them commune with God. It is essentially a how-to guide on prayer that reminds us of some of the things prayer ought to include.

So what are some of the things this prayer includes?

He starts with God. There is adoration and praise and a desire to submit to His will.

The next part is what theologians call supplication. That's the part we know well. It's the asking for stuff part. Even here, Jesus refines our thinking. He prays for daily bread. This is a daily walk with God, not a one and done kind of relationship.

Recall Jesus' teaching on worry?

Read: Matthew 6:31-34

Jesus wants us to stay focused on today.

He also calls us to confess our sins and to forgive others.

Read: 1 John 1:9

What follows is one many today would have trouble praying. They like the forgiveness part, but the prayer to lead me away from temptation is tougher. The current Roman Catholic Pope, in fact, wants to change that line. It's hard for us because we often want to keep doing the sins we just confessed. Praying this line requires us to be honest with God, admit that we want to keep sinning and that we need His help if we are to have any victory there.

After teaching things that might be good for prayer, He teaches us to persist in prayer and to remember that God loves us and gives us good gifts. Our faith grows as we pray.

Closing: Now that you know how to pray—go ahead and do it.

18 MAGICAL?

Open: *Magic Exposed-* If you've ever seen a magician on TV, do you wonder how they did it? Show a clip of or explain/demonstrate how one is done. (https://brightside.me/wonder-curiosities/10-secrets-behind-the-most-famous-magic-tricks-revealed-364360/, https://www.youtube.com/channel/UCkozSCYe1posLlfj UhaJOkw, https://www.youtube.com/watch?v=47SzFpWQiGc.) Often we come up with bizarre explanations that are much more complicated than the reality.

Transition: The Jews thought Jesus was a magician and they had figured out His trick.

Read: Luke 11:14-16

Often when we dislike someone, we can think no good of them. So even if they just donated their kidney to save an orphan, we would find some way to view that negatively. That's where some people were. They hated Jesus so much that they couldn't even acknowledge when He did something wonderful and kind, so they came up with a bizarre excuse to explain what He did.

Here's the problem—their excuse makes no sense. They want to ascribe this miraculous healing to the power of Satan.

Ok. Can you think of any times Satan has healed someone? Need a concordance to locate a verse or two? As you might have guessed—Satan never healed anyone. He is a destroyer, not a healer.

Healing is, rightly, ascribed to God alone.

Read: Exodus 4:11, 2 Kings 5:7, Psalm 41:2-4

The people knew that only God could heal a leper, cast out a demon or give voice to the mute.

Not only that, but this specific type of healing was specifically something the Messiah would do.

Read: Isaiah 35:5-6

Jesus responds to the detractors.

Read: Luke 11:17-23

Jesus not only answers His critics, but points them to what this miracle points to—His kingdom.

This is not Satan's world—this is Christ's kingdom and like a sovereign, He can deport those whom He wishes. These demons are powerless before Him.

This also reminds us that we are powerless to save ourselves. Those afflicted by demons can't make them leave, nor can hard-working friends or relatives. It is accomplished only by the active working of the Lord. The same is true for us.

Closing: You will encounter many people who will hate Jesus and try to take the focus away from what He has done. Don't fall for it! Keep your eyes on Jesus and wonder at His grace.

19 BEST LAID PLANS

Open: *Planning Ahead-* Have you ever seen a sign reading "Coming Soon!" for a project that never really happened (Such as: *Amazing Spiderman 3, Newt* from Pixar, the *District 9* sequel, *Spaceballs 2, Superman Lives, The Golden Compass 2, ET 2*, etc.)? What happened to stop it? They ran out of money, the stock market changed, an actor got arrested, etc. Even worse is a project that was built but never used. Like a factory for a company that went bankrupt or home with many rooms that stood empty due to a car accident.

Transition: Often times, our plans don't work out. God's always do.

Read: Luke 12:13-21

How is this guy any different from Joseph? After-all, the patriarch did much the same thing—built silos to store grain for the coming famine in Egypt. Why do we applaud him and not the rich man?

Jesus does give us a clue in verse 15.

It wasn't the barns that were evil, but the man's attitude of self-reliance and greed. Joseph saw God as provider; this man only saw himself. God was nowhere in his thinking. So he made plans for the future based on his own goals and desires.

That didn't work out so well.

The problem with our plans is that they are our plans. Our plans can fail; God's can't.

Read: Proverbs 19:21

Jesus isn't saying "don't ever plan," but He is challenging us to look to the future in light of our walk with Him and to stop trusting in ourselves.

He also reminds us that He cares for us.

Read: Luke 12: 22-31

No matter what our future holds, we can trust that the Lord will be there for us. We don't need to obsess about what may come or live in fear and anxiety because God loves us. He is going to take care of us.

If we seek first the kingdom, then even when our plans change, we will be okay. God will take care of us.

Unlike the rich man, Joseph had a kingdom focus. That meant building barns and silos because that was God's plan to bless all the people of the region. That was how God was showing his love to His people. That's a very different focus than the selfish one the rich man had.

Closing: What's motivating you as you look forward?

Do you really believe that God cares about you and will provide?

20 GROWING

Open: *Elephant Toothpaste-* Put down a tarp. Put 1 tbsp. of dry yeast into 3 tbsp. of warm water, mix well. Fill a small bottle with ½ cup hydrogen peroxide, some dish soap and food coloring. With a funnel, add the yeast mixture to the bottle. The reaction will happen quickly. (If this is not possible to do the experiment, bring in examples of yeast bread and compare with flat breads such as Matzo or Naan.)

Transition: Adding a little yeast really had a reaction! Jesus said that the kingdom of God is like that, too.

Read: Luke13:18-21

We don't grow a lot of mustard where we are, but we can relate to the idea. Show an acorn or pine nut. These small nuts grow into towering trees.

If you have ever sprouted beans or tried to grow a tomato plant at your house, you know that it takes time for them to develop. Though you might see some quick growth initially, it can take weeks or months for it to be fully grown.

The kingdom of God is like that. It starts small, but grows and grows!

Illustration: At the bottom of the board draw one stick figure. If this one shares the gospel with two people and then each after them does the same, what happens? (Draw each of these until it looks like a very large tree.) It grows exponentially!

The kingdom started in Israel and spread throughout the known world within a few centuries. It always multiplies by person-to- person contact.

The same is true of leaven. It spreads into the whole batch. Then bakers have to proof the bread. That means letting it rise. Afterward, they punch it down and let it rise again so that it can reach full volume. In the same way, the church grows even through adversity.

That was important news for these early believers. They could look forward to the growth even though it was a small crew to begin with.

This also has application to our walk with Christ.

Spiritual maturity takes time. It doesn't happen overnight and it often requires trials to fully develop. But it keeps growing.

It is also interesting that Jesus used the example of a garden tree not a forest one. The mustard seed is tiny and grows into a large bush-like tree, but it is not a sequoia or a towering cedar. That means we probably shouldn't live in disappointment that we aren't spiritual giants. Our faith is supposed to grow deeper and wider as we grow. Part of that is wrestling with our sin and lack of success.

Read: Ephesians 3:17-19

If you are in Christ, you will grow, but don't give up because you think you aren't as holy as someone else.

It's also helpful to realize that the kingdom grows as we interact with our world. We aren't supposed to hide away, but to impact the world with the love of Jesus just as leaven impacts the whole bag of flour.

Closing: The kingdom continues to grow as God's people share His love and grow in relationship with Him.

21 PARTY

Open: *Party Planner-* If you were planning an epic birthday bash, who would you invite? Why? Are there people you might not invite? People you think would show up even if you didn't invite them? (Like distant relatives, your parent's friends, etc.)

Transition: How would you feel if you had that big party but none of the people you invited came?

Read: Luke 14:12-24

You see stories in the news all the time of special children whose parents planned a nice party and invited all the kids in the class, but none showed up. Often times, the happy ending is that policemen, firemen, EMT's or others hear about it and make the day extra special. (Examples: http://www.whio.com/news/firefighters-step-after-one-shows-child-birthday-party/ACB8fT9bLyzlkKhoMTDHCO/, http://www.dailymail.co.uk/news/article-2962916/Osceola-County-cops-flock-autistic-boy-s-birthday-party-mom-Ashlee-Buratti-revealed-none-

classmates-turned-up.html,
htttp://time.com/4797686/dallas-police-attend-birthday-party/)

Jesus told this parable about a similar party. Everyone had excuses why they couldn't make it. They even seem legitimate. Feasts were often big affairs that required travel (Think of a modern day "destination" wedding.) and expense. What you might not realize is that these were people who had already RSVPed that they were attending. The servant was sent out to confirm that things were ready to begin. This would be similar to the parable of the ten virgins from Matthew 25:1-13. They were already there, just waiting for the arrival of the groom. So these folks were not people who couldn't make it, but people who were coming up with reasons not to come.

Who do you think these folks represented? (Jewish leaders, Pharisees, Sadducees, etc.)

God's promises had been given to the Jewish people, yet when Jesus came, those same people weren't interested. They were content in their own righteousness and religiosity.

Read: John 1:11-12

Their apathy and excuses weren't going to stop the party, however. Jesus called the irreligious, the poor, the weak, the broken and the sinful. The gospel is for all who will come.

Read: Matthew 11:28, John 6:37

It's like the child's party: The ones who got the invite weren't the ones who got to eat the cake.

Closing: There are a couple of take-aways here:

1. Don't let your pride or self-righteousness keep you from following Jesus. (And that includes—continuing to walk with Him.)

2. Since the gospel is for everyone, let's invite as many people as we can to the party. (If Jesus could feed 5,000 with a few loaves and fishes, He can make more cake.)

Enjoy the party of the Lamb!

22 SEARCHING

Open: *Lost & Found-* Hide an object in the room. Inform the students that if they find it, they may keep it. How hard would you search if it were just a dollar? Your grandmother's diamond engagement ring? A child?

Transition: To God, you were lost and worth searching for.

Read: Luke 15:1-7

Have you ever lost something? What was it? Did you find it?

In this section, Jesus tells three parables about lost things. The first is about a lost sheep. Whose fault is it that the sheep is lost? (The sheep–it wandered off.)

Why does Jesus tell this story? (The Pharisees objected to Him spending time with sinners.) He equates these people with the lost sheep. Should the shepherd not care for them just because they wandered away? God's love is greater than our sin.

Jesus then tells a story of a woman looking for a lost coin before moving to the parable of the lost son. (Sometimes called the prodigal.)

Read: Luke 15:11-32

This is a story of God's grace. A man's arrogant son asks for his inheritance early. To put it bluntly, he is saying, "Dad, I wish you were dead so I could have my money." He is rejecting his father.

But his father loves him and gives him his portion anyway—which the young man quickly burns through. He is left penniless and working as a lowly pig-herd for a wealthy farmer. Why is that so odd? (This was a Jewish boy and pigs are unclean animals.)

So this young man has rejected his family and his faith.

Even so—when he returns home, hoping merely to be a servant, he is welcomed as a son and restored to a place of honor. He is given grace.

That's where we usually stop the story. So why include the last bit about the other brother? (Answers will vary.)

Read: Vs 7, 10

There is abounding joy when one of these lost ones repents and is saved. Have you ever thought about that before? There is, by contrast, no joy over the self-righteous ones who believe they have no need of repentance. The Pharisees are the second son.

While these are tales of God's mercy, they are also cautionary tales for those who are confident in their own righteousness. They need Jesus just as much as the obviously lost ones.

Closing: So which child are you?

23 YOU SHALL NOT PASS

Open: *Absolute Certainty-* What are things you are certain are true? Why? Many scientific facts, for example, have verifiable evidence to support them. Still, some people are so committed to a wrong idea that they won't give it up despite the facts. Can you think of things like that? (Ex. Flat earth, geo-centric universe, evolution, man-made global warming, etc.)

Transition: Jesus said that some of His listeners were like that.

Read: Luke 16:19-31

Jesus tells a story (And it is a parable, not an actual account, despite the use of the name Lazarus.) of two men. One was poor and ill and desired nothing more than a scrap of leftover food. Most wealthy people did such kindnesses. Recall how Boaz let Ruth and others glean after the harvesters in his fields? This rich man was so selfish, he wouldn't even offer the tiniest bit to Lazarus. (This was, by the way, a common name and does not refer to the raised Lazarus.)

After they die, this selfish man in his torment sees Lazarus afar off. This is a great picture of judgment. The lost can see the joy of the saved but cannot interact with them. There is a division that cannot be crossed between the two.

Read: Hebrews 9:27

Once you pass, you either go to be with the Lord or away from Him. It is also worth noting that this exchange underscores that the Jews did have an understanding of the after-life. Though there were groups, like the Sadducees, that rejected the resurrection, others embraced the idea of a place beyond the grave.

Being unsuccessful in alleviating his discomfort, the man suggests sending Lazarus back to warn his loved ones.

Ironically, this is what happened with Mary & Martha's brother. He was raised from the dead to the amazement of all, yet many still refused to believe.

Abraham tells him that if they would not listen to Moses and the prophets, they would not believe if a man came back from the dead.

What do you think about that?

Some people will not believe no matter what. There are many modern "scholars" who have gone to great lengths to attempt to prove that the miracles of the Bible never happened–the Red Sea was dry due to a drought, Jesus just fainted, the feeding of the 5,000 was just a potluck supper. Even if they met a dead man who was raised to life, they still wouldn't believe.

So what does that tell us? How do men believe?

Read: John 6:36-37, 10:26-29

It is a work of God the Holy Spirit. He is the one who opens hearts and minds. Typically, He uses the Word of God to do so.

Read: 1 Corinthians 1:21

That means we don't have to have the newest, fanciest stuff to attract new converts. It also means we don't have to be the smoothest of talkers in order to share the gospel. It is God who saves, not us, so that takes the pressure off of us.

Closing: If you believe–rejoice that God has opened your eyes to see and believe the truth.

24 THANK YOU

Open: *Thank You Cards-* Jimmy Fallon famously writes thank you cards as a part of the *Tonight Show*. These are often silly like: "thank you, airplane seat by the bathroom, for letting me pay $400 to temporarily live next to an outhouse." (You may share several other examples.)

Try your hand at it. What silly thank you note can you write? Share some.

Transition: People express their thankfulness in many way, but some forget to be thankful at all.

Read: Luke 17:11-19

While being a Samaritan is now associated with being a helpful, kind person, that wasn't always the case. When the Assyrians took the Israelites into captivity, they allowed other peoples to occupy regions like Samaria. Those who did so intermarried with the remaining Jewish people and set up a religion that mixed Judaism and idolatry. They even had their own place of worship separate from Jerusalem. That did not make them popular with the more faithful Jewish people.

So, in essence, Jesus and His disciples are heading toward Jerusalem, but are near the "bad neighborhood" of Samaria.

As they enter a village, 10 lepers call out to them. So not only do you have some of them who are ethnic outcasts here, but they are all also diseased. Leprosy was a term used for lots of skin disorders, many of which were contagious. (See Leviticus 13-14.)

Would you want to go near these men? Care about them?

Let's be honest—it would be super easy to ignore them. In fact, it would have been socially expected to do so. These were unclean people, after all.

Even so—Jesus does acknowledge them and with just a word, heals them. As the law required, He told them to go show themselves to the priest to confirm that they were free from the disease.

One of them, however, turns back and races toward Jesus to thank Him—and he is a Samaritan.

They were all healed, yet only one remembers to thank the healer. The one who was unclean by birth is made clean.

The others were, no doubt, grateful for their healing, but only one really seemed to have an interest in God Himself.

Jesus seems to acknowledge that.

Read: Vs. 19

The Samaritan needed more than a cure from leprosy. His faith has made him well. (Some translations say it saved him.) This is not about being cured of his disease, but being given peace with God, true cleanliness.

Closing: The physical blessings are nice and are worthy of thankfulness, but the greatest gift of salvation is far more valuable.

25 WELCOME TO THE KINGDOM

Open:

Option 1: Are We There Yet? Have you ever gone on a long trip? Did you wonder if you were ever going to get where you were going? Did that make you miss some cool things along the way? Many of the promises of the Bible are now and not yet ones. We see a small fulfillment today, but the best is still to come.

Transition: Jesus reminds us that His kingdom is like that. Knowing that, we can appreciate what we have as we await a greater fulfillment.

Option 2: Multiple Meanings- Can you think of words that have multiple meanings? For example: Love can mean romantic affection, merely liking something ("I love green beans!") or a tennis score. There are lots of words like that, such as: scale, fair, bow, jerk, kid, kind, date, crane, etc. How can you tell which meaning is intended? (By the context.)

Transition: In our passage today, there is a word in the original Greek that could be translated as in, with, around or near. Which do you think Jesus meant?

Read: Luke 17:20-37

Some translators struggle with vs. 21. Instead of saying that the kingdom was in their midst, some chose "within" you. That's a big difference. For example, you'd much rather hear that the flu was in the area than that it was inside you. The Greek word can be used to mean in, with, around, so you have to figure out which English word to use based on context.

How can the context help? Who is Jesus talking to? (Pharisees). Did they believe in Jesus? (No.) So Jesus probably wasn't saying the kingdom lived inside of them, but that it was all around them.

That helps us to realize something else-the kingdom of God is already here.

Does that surprise you?

We often think of the kingdom as future, but it has already begun. Jesus acted as sovereign every time He cast out demons and said things by His own authority. He is ruling.

The kingdom is now, but also not yet. Jesus is expanding His kingdom, growing it, through gospel outreach. Much like a construction project, the final product will be way nicer than what we now see.

The good news is that He is Lord now, destroying the work of Satan.

Read: 1 Corinthians 15:24-26

Having established that Jesus is in charge, He then starts talking about His triumphant return. He uses the Old Testament accounts of Noah and Sodom to remind the people that God always lovingly preserves His people and judges those who turn away from Him. (See the parallel passage in Matthew 24.)

The last section has another one of those words that can mean different things. Vs. 34 talks about 2 people in bed and one is taken. The word bed also refers to the kind of seating used at dinner tables, so it could mean people gathered at a meal or simply asleep.

So why talk about 2 people working and sleeping/eating where one is taken? What is the point? (Answers will vary.)

You aren't okay with God just because you are in a Christian home or are friends with Christians. It's not even enough to be a faithful church-goer like the Pharisees were. We need to actually join the kingdom by placing our faith in Jesus for ourselves. (Switching from the kingdom around us to the kingdom being in us, as it were.)

Otherwise, the picture is of one of judgment.

When the soldiers come, they take away one to punishment (See Matthew 13:24-30) and leave the other in safety.

Closing: Jesus is ruling. Are you one of His subjects or are you a mere observer of His kingdom?

26 GOOD GUY?

Open:

Option 1: Better or Worse? The eye doctor asks that as they adjust your prescription. Let's see what you think about various things. Which is better? Ex. Coke or Pepsi, Grilled Cheese or BLT, Burger or hot dog, Country or Rock, women or men, Honda or Chevy, Red or Blue, You or Hitler?

Transition: Some choices are obvious, but some less so. Are we really that much better than our neighbors?

Option 2: Heroes & Villains- As I list some characters, tell me which is the hero and which is the villain. For example: Batman and Joker; Cain & Abel; Green Goblin & Spiderman; George Washington and King George; Abraham Lincoln & Jefferson Davis; Hitler and Stalin.

Transition: Some of those were easy. Others were not so much. (For example, Stalin was a kind of hero during WWII, but now is known more as a villain.) Today, Jesus tells a story where the hero turns out to be not very heroic.

Read: Luke 18:9-14

If you grew up in first century Israel, you knew all about the Pharisees and unlike today, you would have viewed them with awe and respect. These were the holiest of the holy. They were men who took their spiritual lives seriously. Mom & Dad hoped you would grow up to be one.

Tax collectors, on the other hand, were traitorous scum who took advantage of their own people. It was bad enough that the Romans taxed the Jews heavily, but these Jewish collectors often charged extra taxes as a "fee" of sorts that was used to line their own pockets.

The first hearers of this parable were, no doubt, surprised when Jesus flipped the script and revealed that the hero was actually the villain. (Kind of like the Joker being the good guy instead of Batman.)

So what is the difference between the two men?

Look at the Pharisee for a moment: Is it bad to tithe? Fast? Seek to live a holy life? (No.) So what is the issue? (He was trusting in his own righteousness instead of trusting in the Lord.)

The tax collector, on the other hand, had no illusions of holiness. His only hope was for God to be merciful. That man had a realistic view of himself. He knew his own sin, his own failures, his lack of sufficiency in himself. The Pharisee was arrogantly unaware of his need of the Lord at all.

It can be easier than we'd like to think to fall into the routine of the Pharisee. We can get so caught up in doing things for the Lord that we forget about Him entirely. It's kind of like sending flowers to your girlfriend instead of wanting to actually be with her. That can lead to feeling superior to those who don't do those "holy" things.

Let Jesus bring us all down a peg: The man who knows himself to be a sinner and calls out to Jesus for grace is holier by far than the person who gives millions to missions, teaches Sunday School, sings in the choir, serves as a church officer, attends every service, goes on mission trips but does so forgetting that they are just as vile a sinner in need of a savior.

We are not justified before God by the things we do for Him, but solely by having faith in the completed work of Christ for sinners like us.

Read: Romans 3:20-28

Closing: Are you the hero or the villain? Have you realized your sin and need of a savior or are you trusting in your own righteousness?

27 COME ON IN

Open: *Welcoming Party-* Come up with a cheer to greet the given person– soldier, new mother, missionary, long-lost family member, your enemy.

Transition: The people came out to welcome Jesus, but did they mean it?

Read: Luke 19:28-40

Cultures celebrate differently. American brides wear white, while many Asian brides opt for red. Some celebrate big events by setting off fireworks, shooting cannons, tossing ticker tape, shooting guns or even, hosting a unicorn-themed party with balloons and glitter.

The type of celebration often tells us something about the event itself. What is different about a first birthday party and a 16th (Or 15th in Latin cultures)? How about a 21st? 50th?

Jesus' entry into the city is recorded in all 4 gospels (Matthew 21:8-11, John 12:12-15, Mark 11:1-10), so it must be significant, but it isn't as unique as you might expect. There is a reason it is referred to as "the triumphal entry."

In the first century, there were many city-states. So instead of having large kingdoms with vast lands, a nation might just be a fortified city and the surrounding communities which it protected. So you would have the nations of Pittsburgh and Philadelphia, or in *the Walking Dead* comics/TV show world, Alexandria, Hilltop and the Kingdom. If you conquered one of these city-states, you rode into town and claimed your prize. The Romans had official ceremonies to commemorate such victories called triumphs. The people came out of the city to escort the victor inside. It was symbolic not just of the battle won, but of the people's subjection to the new rule. Sometimes, it was actually welcomed. If their tyrannical leader fell, they often rejoiced upon his defeat. A military victor rode into town wearing a victor's crown on a war horse or chariot with flowers thrown on his path to the cheers of the people.

Compare that with how Jesus enters.

Read: Matthew 21:8-9

There are similar elements (Palm branches, shouting, excitement, the people coming out to welcome him, etc.), but what is different?

One thing has to do with His ride. Luke spends a good bit of time describing this animal.

What do we know about it? (It was a young colt that had never been ridden. John records that it was a donkey colt.) Why do you think Jesus rode a donkey into town?

Jesus was not a military ruler, but there was symbolism to the use of a colt. A warrior rode in on a chariot or war horse to show his power and to remind the masses that he can fight them, if needed. If the people welcomed the ruler and there was no need to put down rebellion, no such symbolism was needed. They could enter on a regular horse. Jesus is so confident of His authority, that He rides in on a young donkey—which would be ceremonially clean and an animal of peace not war. He is not coming to beat down the residents, but to rule with kindness and grace. There is an interesting contrast with His second coming when He is pictured on a war horse. (Revelation 19)

One other thing is different: Jesus is not given a victor's crown, but He will be. The crown of thorns is that victor's crown, even though those who would place it on Him thought otherwise.

As Luke's account closes, he records the Pharisees' objection to the people using the Psalmist's words to refer to Jesus. (Psalm 118:26) Instead of rebuking His followers, He rebukes these supposed holy men by telling them that even rocks know that Jesus is the Messiah.

Closing: Jesus is the victorious king, but a king of peace, mercy and grace. Have you welcomed Him as your savior and Lord or will you let the stones do your job for you?

28 IT'S A TRAP!

Open:

Option 1: Things You Don't Like to Do- What are some things you don't like to do, but you have to do anyway? (Go to school, doctor, practice, do homework, eat veggies, etc.) Why do you do them?

Transition: Jesus calls upon us to sometimes do things that don't seem enjoyable, but which serve a purpose.

Option 2: It's a Trap! Show several examples of traps. (Such as mouse traps, Venus Fly Traps, Chinese finger puzzle, etc.) Is there a way to safely navigate these without getting caught? (You can also set up a "laser" challenge using string tied in various positions to see if it is possible to navigate from one side to the other without touching a "laser" and getting caught.) Allow students to find creative ways to escape traps. Why do people set such traps anyway? (They want to get rid of something that annoys them.)

Transition: The Pharisees really didn't like Jesus, so they set a trap.

Read: Luke 20:19-26

One thing almost everyone agrees on is that they hate taxes. That's why politicians always talk about cutting taxes when campaigning for office even when they don't really intend to do so.

It should come as no surprise, then, that first century people hated them, too. So the Pharisees decide to set a trap for Jesus.

Have you heard about the old lawyer trick? They ask a yes/no question like, "Have you stopped beating your wife?" If you answer "yes," it means you did beat her; if you answer "no" it means you are still beating her. There is no good answer.

This question is similar. If Jesus says believers should pay taxes, the Jews will dislike Him; if he says not to, the Romans will hate him.

Jesus doesn't fall for their trap, but instead asks them a question: Whose face is on the money they use?

By using the coins, they are tacitly agreeing to the rules governing them, including taxes.

Though this was in response to a trick, it is worth noting that Jesus is calling upon believers to be good citizens of their countries. Paul expands on the idea.

Read: Romans 13:1-7

By submitting to those is rightful authority over us, we glorify the Lord and provide a good testimony to unbelievers.

That means that even though taxes are often high and are used wastefully, as good citizens, we ought to render unto our leaders what is lawfully due them.

The flipside of that is that we also ought to render to God what is God's. The Jews would have naturally thought of the tithe, but it also includes using our gifts and talents for the Lord.

Closing: Don't fall into the trap of thinking you don't need to engage with your community. Be a good citizen, but also use your gifts for the Lord, too.

29 20 QUESTIONS

Open: *Quiz Show*- Set teams up, but ask 2 questions at a time. (One very hard; one a bit easier. Such as: How many gospels are there? How many total verses are in John?) Allow them to decide which they want to answer.

Transition: How would you do if you had to answer both? Jesus faces that situation today.

Read: Luke 21:5-27

Oftentimes, when young kids get excited, they rattle off a bunch of questions. "When do we go to Disney? Will it be soon? Will we drive or fly? Who is coming with us? What are we having for dinner tonight?"

Natural excitement can lead even adults to do that. So when the disciples hear Jesus talk about the destruction of the temple, their ears perk up and they want to know what He is talking about and if it means something more.

Luke records them asking two questions, but Matthew mentions that they asked another, too. (Gospel writers often included different details in their accounts. This is similar to how 2 different attenders can hear the same speech, but one focuses on one portion and another emphasizes a different point.)

Read: Matthew 24:3

The temple was a sacred place and even these young believers realized it was a big deal if it were to fall. They knew their history and that it had been destroyed by invaders before. They definitely didn't want to be around when that happened again.

There was also the deeper question of what this fall might mean for Jesus and His followers.

So Jesus responds to the questions they asked and ones they may not have, but needed to know. In essence, He is open about what will happen, but makes sure to comfort them with the knowledge that He has got this. He is still in charge.

Because He answers several questions, some readers can get confused. Which things apply to each event? (The fall of Jerusalem, destruction of the temple and the return of Christ.)

Much of this section seems to point to the fall of Jerusalem. What would lead to that conclusion? (In Luke's gospel he doesn't record the disciples asking about the end of the age, so most of what lists would be responses to the main questions he is dealing with. The advice given only seems relevant to an earthly event like the fall of a city. We know historically that these things did occur prior to 70 AD.)

At verse 25, however, Jesus signals a turn to what

happens after that horrible event. His followers needed to know there is more to the story than the coming sadness.

Read: Vs. 25-27

What does this focus on? (The coming of Jesus in glory.)

Read: 1 Thessalonians 4:16-17

It's the second triumphal entry!

Jesus is open and honest with His disciples about what is to come–including unimaginable things like the temple and Jerusalem falling, but in the midst of that He reminds them that He is still in charge and He has a plan.

Closing: Are there times you need to hear that? When stuff is not going well in your life and hope is a luxury, remember that Jesus has got this. He still loves you; He still has a plan. In the end it all work out for His glory and your good.

30 ONE OF THESE THINGS IS NOT LIKE THE OTHER

Open:

Option 1: Similar- Show 2 pictures. (You can use Highlights Magazine-style ones or just two pictures of similar things like 2 football teams.) How are they similar? How are they different?

Transition: The meal Jesus shares with His disciples is both similar and different from our communion.

Option 2: Same? How are the given items the same? How are they different? Ex. Cheetah and leopard, Great Dane and German Shepherd, Christmas dinner and Thanksgiving dinner, soccer and hockey, shoes and sandals, etc.

Transition: The meal Jesus shares with His disciples is both similar and different from our communion.

Read: Luke 22:14-23

I'm betting Jewish moms didn't tell their kids to sit up straight at the table. Why? Their tables were different from ours. They were very low and people reclined on cushions in order to eat. So even though this was a very formal meal, everyone was reclining at the table.

What do you know about Passover? (Answers will vary.)

This was one of the biggest Jewish holidays. It is similar to Thanksgiving in that it involved a huge family meal that expressed thankfulness to God. It was celebrated every year as a remembrance of how God rescued His people during the Exodus.

The meal was very symbolic and included lamb, flat bread, herbs, egg, sweet wine and more. Each element was used to teach part of the story of the Exodus.

It was a special occasion and one most people looked forward to. Jesus did, too. He was excited to share the past with His friends, but also to look toward the future.

While enjoying the meal together, he focused in on two of the items on the table—the bread and the wine. Why do you think He chose these? (Answers will vary.) They were both simple symbols of the death He would soon die that could serve as good reminders of it, also.

Read: 1 Corinthians 11:23-26

For us, these items are done in remembrance of Christ's completed work on the cross for us. The flat bread symbolizes His body and the cup His blood. Jesus uses the word covenant to describe it. Do you know what a covenant is? (A solemn agreement, contract, a formal promise.)

The fact that Jesus went to that cross is a sure sign that His promises are good. He did what it took to save us. So when He says we are forgiven—we are!

Closing: Even though these passages relate specifically to the communion meal at worship, each time you eat some bread or drink, you can use that to remind you of what your savior did out of love for you and be reminded that His promises to you are true.

31 I'D NEVER DO THAT!

Open: *Why I'd Never!*- What are some things you'd never do? (Drink Pepsi, eat my dog, cheat on my significant other, eat at McDonald's, etc.) Can you think of a situation where you might do that anyway? (Such as drinking Pepsi when you are dying of thirst and it's the only option.)

Transition: Peter would never deny Jesus. . . or maybe he would.

Read: Luke 22:31-34, 54-62

People sometimes find themselves doing things they can't imagine they would ever do—like cheating, stealing, lying, turning on a friend. Peter and Jesus were great friends and it was inconceivable to Peter to think that he would ever reject that relationship. So it was surprising to hear Jesus say that Peter would do just that.

Soon after Peter's boast, the inconceivable happens and Peter denies Jesus 3 times!

Notice some things about this which are just awesome:

1. Jesus knew that Peter would deny Him.

2. Jesus loved him anyway.

3. That love led Peter to real repentance and forgiveness.

However you sinned this week–it didn't come as a surprise to Jesus. He knows everything about you. Amazingly, just like with Peter, that doesn't make Him reject you. He still loves you.

When you read verse 61, Jesus turns to look at Peter and Peter immediately responds with remorse. I don't think it was one of those "gotcha" looks that teachers and parents are famous for. It wasn't a look to say you are busted, but a look that says to Peter: "I'm not going anywhere. I don't reject you."

Closing: Remember that is how Jesus views you and respond as Peter did in repentance.

32 NOT GUILTY

Open:
Option 1: Injustice Files- Share real stories of people wrongly convicted. (Many available online.)

Transition: Despite declaring Him innocent, the judge still sentenced Jesus to die.

Option 2:That's Not Fair! Can you think of a situation where someone was treated really unfairly–like a bad call by a ref, your sibling gets a bigger piece of cake than you, a teacher who punishes the whole class for one person's actions or a criminal who didn't get justice?

Transition: While those are bad, there is an act of injustice that is even greater.

Option 3: Making a Murderer- If you were doing a podcast about the trial of Jesus, what things could you point to that would prove He was innocent of a crime?

Transition: Despite being innocent, He was still treated as if He were guilty.

Read: Luke 23:13-25

How do trials work in our country? (Innocent until proven guilty, sworn testimony, evidence is provided, guilt must be proven, etc.) Once a person is found not guilty, what do we do with them? (Free them.) So why wasn't Jesus freed?

This wasn't an act of justice, but of politics. The Jews wanted Jesus dead, but they weren't permitted by Rome to execute prisoners. The Roman leaders had to decide if that was to be permitted. That's where it got tricky. It would be easier on the governor to go with the will of the Jewish leadership in order to keep them on his side. It made good sense. But even he was surprised that they would want to execute Jesus. He declared, in agreement with Herod, that there was zero evidence of wrong-doing by Jesus.

Even so, he didn't want to ruffle feathers.

What were his options here? What could he do to save face for him and the Jewish leadership?

There was a perfect option that Pilate tries to employ.

Read: John 18:38-39

As an act of good will, the territorial governor would release/pardon a prisoner during the annual Passover holiday. Pilate thought that the Jews could request that Jesus be freed so they would appear gracious despite having wrongly accused Jesus.

His gamble failed. They chose an actual criminal to be released—Barabbas, instead of Jesus.

We look at Pilate and see a guy who could have done the right thing–he had the authority to do so, but decided to go with the crowd instead. It was just easier.

There's a lesson there. But there's also the reminder that religious people can be united in the wrong things. Just because a group thinks something is true, that doesn't always make it so. That's why we are challenged to test everything by scripture. That is something those leaders failed to do.

Closing: It is a sad thing when politics trumps truth, but it happens all too often. You may not be able to change the world around you, but you can at least take a stab at doing the right thing yourself.

33 THIS AIN'T ROCKET SCIENCE

Open:
Option 1:The Hard Way- Ask students to come up with an unnecessarily difficult way to do a simple task. (Such as tying shoes, making a sandwich, sharpening a pencil, etc.)

Transition: You can make some things very complicated, but don't make the gospel one of them.

Option 2: Rube Goldberg- Have you heard of a Rube Goldberg machine? Goldberg was a cartoonist know for drawing insanely complicated machines to do simple tasks. (*Back to the Future* includes examples of such machines. You can show a clip, if you like.) Share examples of these crazy machines. (Samples at: http://coolmaterial.com/roundup/rube-goldberg-machines/ or http://mentalfloss.com/article/54007/8-excellent-rube-goldberg-cartoons)

Transition: You can make some things very complicated, but don't make the gospel one of them.

Read: Luke 23:26-43

What do you need to do to be saved?

People have many different answers to that. Some think you must be baptized or be confirmed in a church; that you must do more good than bad in your life; you must be able to explain the basic beliefs of your church or just pray a prayer to Jesus, whether you mean it or not.

People who believe that way are often gummed up by this passage. Why? Because Jesus says to a convicted criminal being crucified next to Him that he would be with Jesus in heaven. There is no mention of baptism, church membership or any other things. In fact, all we do know that he is a man who, by his own testimony, deserved the punishment he was receiving and that he called to Jesus to remember him.

So in answer to the question, what must I do to be saved, Jesus makes it clear—it isn't that complicated.

Read: Acts 16:30-31

Paul makes it clear, too—believe in Jesus and you will be saved. Nothing else is necessary.

So what does that mean? What does it mean to believe?

We often use the acrostic KAT to unpack that. One must *know* certain things such as that sin exists and deserves punishment and that God exists. They must also *agree* that those thing apply to them. (*I* am a sinner. *I* need Jesus to save me.) The last is to *trust* in Jesus alone. That's harder than just knowing facts.

Let's consider the thief. Did he believe like that? (It

seems so. He knew what was said about Jesus. He knew himself to be a sinner that needed Jesus to save him. He asked Jesus for help.)

So if that man was saved, what does that tell us?

Think you have to have your stuff together to be saved? The thief didn't.

Think you need to know the whole Bible to be saved? The thief didn't.

Think you have to be baptized or join a church in order to be saved? The thief didn't.

It's not a bad thing to desire personal holiness, to know the Bible or to connect with a church, but those *flow out of your relationship with Jesus, they don't make you have a relationship with Him.* Don't complicate faith by adding conditions to it. Simply believe. And encourage others to do the same.

Closing: Have you done that? If not, you can trust Jesus today. If you have, grow in your relationship with Him in the same way—by faith.

34 REACTIONS

Open: *Different Reactions-* How do you respond to the following stories? Share current events items. Do you have a strong reaction, no reaction or just indifference?

Transition: People reacted in different ways to the resurrection, too.

Read: Luke 24:1-12

Have you ever noticed how small children respond to new things? Some cling in terror to Mom's legs; others run and explore, some laugh or look perplexed.

Jesus' friends had similarly different reactions to the news of His resurrection.

To set the scene: It is early Sunday morning, the start of the week. As was customary, the women bring spices to place on Jesus' body. This was to lessen the smell from decay, so that visitors, who often had to travel from a distance, could grieve without being knocked over by the odor. They are surprised by two things: 1. There are no guards there and 2. Jesus is gone. Two angels meet them to share the good news of His resurrection and to remind them that Jesus had told them this would happen. In their grief, they had forgotten this. (*Note:* Matthew and Mark only note one angel at the tomb. This is not a contradiction. By way of illustration: It is similar to going to a rally. When asked about it, one person might note what the candidate said. A reporter might, however, include that info as well as the fact that two council members, the mayor and a community group leader also spoke. Luke is acting more like a reporter here.)

How did they react? (They left immediately to share the good news with the disciples. The resurrection motivated them to action.)

How did most of the disciples greet the information? (With disbelief.) They thought this was all a bunch of wishful thinking or idle chatter. (Like debating who would win a fight between Superman and the Hulk.) The resurrection inspired disbelief in some.

What about Peter? (He ran to the tomb.) Why do you think he did that? (To see if it could be true.) It's ironic that the one who rejected Jesus was one of the first to race to His tomb. For some, the resurrection inspires hope. If Jesus were alive, Peter could hope for forgiveness and restoration.

Think about this for a bit. How do you react? Does Christ's resurrection give you hope? Motivate you to action? Or are you indifferent and disbelieving? Those are questions worth asking yourself. The resurrection matters.

Read: 1 Corinthians 15:12-19

That event is the confirmation that our debt has been

paid. It is our receipt that we are truly forgiven and our motivation to live a new life.

Read: Luke 7:47

Love much because you were loved so well.

It also helps us to understand how others see things. Our unsaved friends are utterly befuddled by the resurrection. They don't believe it or see how it could possibly matter. It is easier to ignore it or treat it as a fairy tale than to deal with it. Allow your belief in the resurrection to give you hope that God can open their eyes, too.

Closing: Jesus has been raised? What is your reaction?

35 ON THE ROAD

Open: *Where's Waldo?* Share one or more *Where's Waldo* puzzles. Can you find him in the picture? Once you see him, it's hard not to see him, right?

Transition: Once the Messiah came, it was hard not to see Him in all of scripture.

Read: Luke 24:13-35

Have you ever gone on a journey? Did you notice how frequently you ended up having long, deep conversations with people during the trip? These particular folks were walking from Jerusalem to Emmaus (Around 7 miles.). To kill time they struck up a conversation with a stranger.

Even though their conversation was about Jesus, doesn't it seem odd that they didn't recognize Him? The text tells us that they were kept from doing so (verse 16), but that probably wasn't that odd anyway. Most people would have only seen Jesus in large crowds. (Imagine seeing a favorite band from the nosebleed seats with no

Jumbo Tron. It would be hard to recognize them later.)

The two friends are perplexed about what happened in Jerusalem to Jesus and talk to the stranger about it. After a brief recap, he does something amazing and starts showing how the Old Testament pointed to Jesus–including how He died.

If you have ever seen a movie mystery or a film like *the Sixth Sense* and get to the big reveal at the end; the next time you watch it, you see all the clues you missed the first time.

Jesus takes them through the Old Testament to show them what they had missed. What do you think He could have pointed to? (Answers will vary)

We aren't given the list, but He might have talked about some of these:

Read: Genesis 3:15, Isaiah 53, Psalm 22:1,14-18

Why does it matter?

There are many reasons, but some might include that it encouraged these believers that this was always a part of God's plan, that Jesus was, indeed, the promised Messiah, that the resurrection was true, that Jesus cared.

That last part was especially true. As they sat down to eat, Jesus allowed them to really see Him. He was there for them. They may never have been that close to Him before, but He chose to travel with them and meet them in their sadness. He cared.

Their response is amazing, too. They went back immediately. Despite having already walked 7 miles and darkness was setting in, they had to share the good news.

Closing: Jesus is not a New Testament person only. He has always existed and is spoken of regularly throughout the Old Testament. Be encouraged that He chose to reveal Himself to you.

36 GHOST STORY?

Open:

Option 1: Gift Registry- If you were getting married, what might you want? How about for a birthday? Are there gifts you'd like, but you can't buy, like athletic ability, popularity, etc.?

Transition: Jesus gives His disciples a surprising gift that they couldn't get on their own.

Option 2: Ghost Stories- Have you heard any good "ghost stories?" Share several examples from pop culture. (*The Sixth Sense, the Conjuring* films, *Sleepy Hollow* or even *Casper.*) Are these true stories? Why not? (Ghosts aren't real.)

Transition: Today starts off like a such a story when the disciples think Jesus is a ghost, but He shows them He is real.

Read: Luke 24:36-53

Like today, there were many superstitious people in the first century. They told stories of ghosts and spirits all the time. So when Jesus suddenly appears to the disciples as they are talking about the Emmaus road experience, they assume He is a ghost. They had the same reaction when they saw Him walk on the water. (Matthew 14:26) They had no box in their brain to check off to fit the kind of things Jesus did. (Like being raised from the dead.)

But Jesus was not a disembodied spirit. He was real. In fact, He goes out of His way to prove it. He shows them His scarred hands and feet and even goes so far as to eat some fish. (*Ghostbusters* taught us that ghosts can't eat without it passing through them.)

Why do you think Jesus did this? Why did it matter? (Answers will vary.)

There are many reasons, but they may include that it proved He was actually raised, not just "spiritually;" that God's plan includes the physical; that He retained His humanity even post-resurrection, etc.

Interestingly, several heretical movements arose in the centuries afterward that rejected the physical aspect of Jesus' resurrection.

Jesus was not a ghost, but a real, physical person.

And He had good news.

Read: Vs 49

He was giving them a gift and this gift was a spirit. He was going to give them the Holy Spirit. Why?

He just gave them a difficult, if not impossible, task to be His witnesses throughout the world. They didn't have the power to do that, but God the Holy Spirit does.

God never calls us to do something that He does not also equip us to do. They would need His help.

Having encouraged them, given them hope and assigned them a task, He ascended to heaven.

Closing: As Luke closes his gospel, he reminds us that Jesus came for a purpose. He came, as was prophesied, to pay the penalty for our sins and to give us new life. He also has called us to share that good news with others. If you have been transformed by His grace, go ahead and tell someone.

ABOUT THE AUTHOR

Eric Dugan has spent over 30 years ministering to students and adults as a pastor, youth pastor, teacher and camp director. He is a Presbyterian Church in America pastor with a BA in Biblical Studies from Geneva College and an MA in Theology from Reformed Theological Seminary. He can't dance, but he can sing. There is video to prove it. Sad, embarrassing video. You can connect with him on Facebook at ERGministryresources or at ericaterg@gmail.com.

Made in the USA
Monee, IL
23 November 2021